Basic Troubleshooting
For The New
Fire 8

Table of Contents

Basic troubleshooting for the New Kindle 8

Hello too all the millions of Amazon Kindle users. Kindle is a great product but sometimes has it problems. So I made this e book to make it easier for all the Kindle users out there to troubleshoot their device before calling Amazon Kindle support which does an awesome job but whose wants to spend a lot of time on the phone. This e book will cover the New Kindle 8. This e book will cover screen issues, wireless issues, and apps issues and much more so let's get started.

A Little Information to Know

- Before doing any trouble shooting on your devices make sure the battery is charged up to at least 40% or more.

- The number to Kindle support is 1-866-321-8851

- Before resetting your device to factory default settings contact Kindle support so they can get information off the device in case further troubleshooting is needed.

  When doing a hard reset of the device hold the power button for at least 30 – 45 seconds to make sure the device resets.

- You want to make sure your Kindle always has the most recent software updates. Use the help pages on www.amazon.com to see if you have the most recent updates.

- With some wireless issues make sure you have the correct password sometimes they can be enter wrong so just double check to be sure. If you see a white x next to the wife symbol that means that there is an issue with your router. Kindle support cannot troubleshoot routers you much contact the company or person who install it for you to check the settings in the router.

This eBook is also available in paperback.

Settings Basics

Quick Actions

Swipe down from the top of the screen to show Quick Actions:

1. **Brightness - Adjust the screen brightness.**
2. **Wireless - Connect to a wireless network.**
3. **Airplane Mode - To turn off all Connectivity.**
4. **Bluetooth device - Pair other Bluetooth devices.**
5. **Do Not Disturb - Mutes all alerts.**
6. **Camera – Turns on camera.**
7. **Help - Access to the on-device Help and Amazon Customer Service contact.**
8. **Screen Rotate- -Turn screen rotation on and odd.**

9. **Settings** - Access additional device settings, such as the date and time, parental controls, keyboards, accessibility options.

Settings Menu

1. **Sync and Check for New Items**
2. **My Account**
3. **Help**
4. **Household Profiles**
5. **Wireless &VPN**
6. **Device Options**
7. **Power Management**
8. **Applications**
9. **Keyboard**
10. **Language**
11. **Accessibility**
12. **Notifications & Quiet Time**
13. **Parental Controls**
14. **Security & Privacy**
15. **Legal & Compliance**

Fire Tablet Basics
Manage Sounds and Notifications

You can view and modify notifications from Quick Actions or mute notifications using Quiet Time on your Fire Tablet.

Note: Your device will sound when you plug it in, when it's fully charged, and when you press and hold the power button to turn off your device. These notifications cannot be turned off.

1. To view a notification, swipe down from the top of the screen to open Quick Actions.
2. Your notification will appear below the Quick Actions menu. Tap the notification to interact with it, or swipe the notification to dismiss it. To dismiss multiple notifications, tap Clear All.

Note: You can also view and dismiss notifications on from the lock screen. Swipe down from the top of the lock screen to view, tap into, or dismiss a notification. To turn off this feature, swipe down from the top of the screen, tap Settings, and then tap Security & Privacy. Next to Lock Screen Notifications, tap Off.

3. **To modify settings for notifications:**
   - **Press and hold the notification to quickly manage settings for that application.**
   - **Swipe down from the top of the screen, and then tap Settings. Tap Notifications & Quiet Time, and then select an app from the list to allow the app to appear in the notification tray or play a sound when a notification arrives for that app.**

Tip: Quiet Time mutes all notification sounds and hides notifications. To turn on Quiet Time, tap Quiet Time from Quick Actions. You can schedule Quiet Time to automatically turn on during a certain time period or whenever you are doing certain activities on the device, like reading a book or listening to music.

Access Your Content

Your Fire Tablet can store thousands of books, apps, games, music, videos, and more, which are referred to as "content" throughout our Help pages. There are several ways to access, organize, and remove content from your device. Connect to a wireless network to sync your items or download content from the Cloud to your Fire Tablet.

Sync your Fire Tablet

Sync your Fire Tablet to receive content from the Amazon Cloud, synchronize content progress across devices, and download any updates.

1. Swipe down from the top of the screen and then tap **Settings**.
2. Tap **Sync and Check for New Items**.

Download content from the Cloud

After you purchase Kindle content, it is saved to the Cloud. When you connect to a wireless network, you can download items from the Cloud to your Fire Tablet.

From **Home**, tap a content library (for example, **Books**) in the top navigation bar.

1. Tap a title to download it to your device. Items that have been downloaded to your Fire Tablet display a check mark in the lower right corner of the cover image. Items that are stored in the Cloud do not display a check mark.
2. Tap the title to open it.

Battery Management

Manage your battery usage or enable Smart Suspend to automatically preserve power on your Fire Tablet.

Adjust notification settings	Swipe down from the top of the screen and tap **Settings**, and then tap **Notifications & Quiet Time**. Choose an application from the list, or tap **Quiet Time** to disable notification alerts.

Lower screen brightness	Swipe down from the top of the screen and then tap **Brightness**. Use the roller bar to lower the brightness. **Tip:** Tap **On** next to **Auto-Brightness** to allow your device to automatically adjust the brightness settings depending on your surroundings. This feature is not available on all devices.
Turn off wireless	Swipe down from the top of the screen and then tap **Wireless**. Next to **Airplane Mode**, tap **On**.
Use headphones	Plug headphones into the headphone jack next to the volume buttons to avoid extended use of the audio speakers on your Fire Tablet.
Adjust screen timeout	Swipe down from the top of the screen and then tap **Settings**. Tap **Display & Sounds**, and then tap **Display Sleep** to select the time it takes for your Fire Tablet to go into sleep mode when you're not using it.
Reduce the inbox check frequency for the Email app	Swipe down from the top of the screen and then tap **Settings**. Tap **Applications**, and then tap **Email, Contacts, and Calendars**. Select your e-mail account, and then tap **Inbox check frequency** to change how frequently your Inbox checks for new e-mails.

Smart Suspend

You can enable Smart Suspend to automatically or manually manage your device's battery power. Smart Suspend will turn off Wi-Fi and other connectivity when you are not using your device.

By default, Smart Suspend is set to automatically learn the right times to turn off Wi-Fi (when you are not typically using your device) in order to preserve power.

Tap AUTOMATIC to tell your device when you want it to turn Wi-Fi off.

To turn off Smart Suspend:

1. Swipe down from the top of the screen and tap Settings, and then tap Power Management.
2. Next to Smart Suspend, tap OFF.

CONNECT WIRELESSLY

Turn On Airplane Mode

Turn off your wireless connection when you are not using it on your Fire Tablet.

Connect to Bluetooth

You can pair your Fire Tablet with wireless devices that use Bluetooth technology, such as speakers, keyboards, or mouse.

Note: Bluetooth microphones, microphone-enabled headsets, and low energy devices are not supported.

1. Verify that your Bluetooth accessory is turned on and set to pairing mode.
2. On your Fire Tablet, swipe down from the top of the screen and then tap Wireless.
3. Tap Bluetooth.
4. Next to Bluetooth, tap on.
5. Tap Pair a Bluetooth Device. A list of available Bluetooth devices will appear.
6. Tap a Bluetooth accessory to pair it with your Fire Tablet, and then follow any additional pairing instructions. After you pair your Bluetooth accessory with your device, a Bluetooth ✳ indicator will appear next to the wireless indicator in the top right corner of

the screen. If the Bluetooth indicator is grey ⁎, your device is not paired with your Bluetooth accessory.

Second Screen on Fire Tablet

You can use Second Screen to connect your Fire tablet to the Amazon Video app on your Amazon Fire TV, Fire TV Stick, or PlayStation console.

Your TV acts as the primary viewing screen, while your Fire tablet goes into companion mode. You can then use your tablet as a remote to control video playback, or as a customized display for X-ray so you can learn more about the movie or TV show you're watching. You can also quickly browse the web, view your email, and more.

Second Screen is currently supported on the following devices:

. Fire phone

- Fire HD 6 (4th Generation)
- Fire HD 7 (4th Generation)
- Fire HDX 8.9 (4th Generation)
- Kindle Fire HDX (3rd Generation)
- Kindle Fire HD (3rd Generation)
- Kindle Fire (2nd Generation)
- Kindle Fire HD (2nd Generation)
- Amazon Fire TV
- Fire TV Stick
- PlayStation 3 (PS3)
- PlayStation 4 (PS4)

Tip: Before you begin, make sure your Fire tablet and Second Screen device are turned on and connected to the Internet. You can use separate wireless, Wi-Fi, or wired Internet connections, as long as the Second Screen device and your tablet can both connect to the Internet at the same time.

1. From your Fire tablet, tap Videos, and then tap Store. Use the Search bar to find the movie or TV show you want to watch.

2. From the video's details, tap the Second Screen ⊕ icon.
3. In the window that appears, select a Second Screen device to send the movie or TV show. If you see (offline) next to the device, make sure the Amazon Video application is open on that device.

Your movie or TV show will load and begin playing on your selected device. While watching, you can control playback of the video on your Fire tablet using the Play▸, Pause❙❙, or Jump Back ↺ buttons onscreen. You can also use the video progress bar to move forward or go back.

If the movie or TV show includes X-Ray, tap In Scene to see synchronized actor, character, trivia, and music information.

Note: The In Scene option is not available for all movies and TV shows that include X-Ray.

When you're finished watching, tap the Second Screen ⊕ icon again, and then select your Fire tablet to end playback on your connected device.

QUICK FIXES

Basic Troubleshooting for Fire Tablet

Try these troubleshooting steps for resolving issues on your Fire Tablet, like a frozen screen, app errors, or problems with content.

Frozen screen or unresponsive device	If the screen on your Fire Tablet is frozen, or your device is unresponsive in general, restart it.
	Press and hold the Power button for 40 seconds or until the device restarts automatically. If your device restarts automatically before 40 seconds has passed, release the Power button. If your device does not automatically restart after 40 seconds, press the Power button to turn it on.
Problems purchasing or accessing content	Confirm that your device is connected to the Internet, either through Wi-Fi or through a mobile connection, such as 4G, if enabled for your device. Your device must be connected to the Internet to buy and sync content or to download content from the Cloud.
	Check the status of your Wi-Fi or mobile connection from the status bar at the top of the screen. The **Wi-Fi** icon will indicate the strength of your wireless connection. A mobile connection will show LTE, 4G, 3G, EDGE, or GPRS.
	If you are in an area with a poor Wi-Fi signal, try turning it off and back on, or selecting a different Wi-Fi network.

Purchased or downloaded content not appearing	Verify that your device is registered to the correct Amazon account.
	• To verify your registration, swipe down from the top of the screen and tap **Settings** and then tap **My Account**. If you see the wrong account listed, tap **Deregister**, and then tap **Deregister** again to confirm. After you deregister your device, tap **Register** to register your Fire Tablet to the correct account.
	If your device is registered to the correct account, confirm that your device is connected to a Wi-Fi or mobile network. Then, swipe down from the top of the screen and tap **Sync and Check for New Items**.
	Note: Content over 50MB can't be downloaded over a mobile network connection.
Specific app issues	Swipe down from the top of the screen and then tap **Settings**, tap **Applications**, and then tap **Manage All Applications**. If you don't see the application you want to manage, tap the **Third-Party Applications** drop-down and select **All Applications**. Select the application you want to manage. You can clear data, clear cache, force stop, or uninstall the application if you are having problems with it.
	Note: Amazon applications, such as Silk, cannot be uninstalled from your device.
	If you clear data, it won't delete the app; however, saved information such as game scores or account information may be lost or need to be re-entered.
	Tip: Quickly force stop an app by accessing the **Quick Switch** panel. From any screen, with the exception of the home screen, swipe from the options bar to the center of the screen. Swipe any item to the center of the screen to force stop the application.

Battery Doesn't Charge

If your Fire Tablet doesn't charge, follow these steps.

Before you begin, make sure that:

1. **You are using the power adapter and micro-USB cable that came with your device.**

2. **You are charging your device from a power outlet. Using a USB port connected to a computer will increase charging time.**

3. **The micro-USB cable is securely connected to your device and power adapter.**

Then:

1. **Unplug the power adapter and micro-USB cable from your device, and then connect them to your device again.**

2. **Insert the power adaptor into a power outlet.**

3. **If your device doesn't indicate that it's charging, unplug the power adapter. Press and hold the Power button for 40 seconds or until the device restarts automatically. If your device restarts automatically before 40**

seconds has passed, release the Power button. If your device does not automatically restart after 40 seconds, press the Power button to turn it on.

4.After you restart (or attempt to restart) your device, plug the power adapter and micro-USB cable into the device and charge for at least an hour.

If your device is turned on, the battery indicator will look like this when your Fire Tablet is charging.

If your device's sound is turned on, a sound will indicate when a charger connects

If your Fire Tablet doesn't turn on or doesn't respond, make sure the power adapter and micro-USB cable are securely connected, and verify that your electrical outlet is working.

Can't Connect to Wi-Fi

If you can't connect to a Wi-Fi network on your Fire Tablet, follow these steps.

Before you begin, make sure that:

1. Other devices in your home can connect to your network. If they can't connect, you may need to contact your Internet service provider for additional help.

2. Airplane Mode is off. To check, swipe down from the top of the screen and tap Wireless. If Airplane Mode is On, tap Off to enable wireless connectivity.

3. You know your Wi-Fi password. If you've forgotten or don't know your Wi-Fi password, you may need to refer to your router manufacturer or Internet service provider for additional help.

4. Your device is on the latest software version. You can install the latest software version wirelessly if you're able to connect to a more stable network, or download and

transfer the software update to your device via USB.

Then:

1. Restart your Wi-Fi connection on your device. Swipe down from the top of the screen and tap Wireless, and then tap Wi-Fi. Next to Wi-Fi, tap Off. After you turn off your Wi-Fi connection, tap On to turn it on again.

2. Restart your device. Press and hold the Power button for 40 seconds or until the device restarts automatically. If your device restarts automatically before 40 seconds has passed, release the Power button. If your device does not automatically restart after 40 seconds, press the Power button to turn it on.

3. Move closer to your router. From your device, check if you can connect to your Wi-Fi network. If your network doesn't appear in the list, tap Scan from the Wi-Fi menu. If you

still don't see your preferred network, you can add it manually to your device. To learn more, go to <u>Add a Wi-Fi Network Manually</u>.

4. Restart your router and modem. Unplug your modem and router, wait a full 30 seconds, and then plug the modem in. After your modem turns on, plug in your router and wait for it to turn on.

If you still can't connect to your network, or you still have limited connectivity, refer to your Internet service provider for additional help.

Quick Fix: Slow or Frozen Screen

If your Fire or Kindle screen is slow to respond or freezes, restart your device or try the troubleshooting steps below.

Troubleshooting Slow Screen Response

Below are some potential reasons you might experience a slow or unresponsive Fire or Kindle screen. Follow the troubleshooting

steps to optimize your device screen performance.

Potential Issue	Troubleshooting Steps
Low battery	If your device battery is low, charge your device for at least 30 minutes, and then try restarting again
Previous software version	Make sure you have the latest software version for your device. To learn more, go to Fire & Kindle Software Updates and select your device to find the latest software update.
Download in progress	If you are currently downloading content on your device, it may be slow to respond until all downloads are complete. It may also be slow immediately after downloading a large amount of content.
Device temperature	Avoid using your device in extreme hot or cold temperature conditions.
Device accessories	If you have a protective case or screen, try removing it and testing the device without it.
Touchscreen is dirty	Clean the screen with a soft, slightly damp, lint-free cloth. Avoid using the device while wearing gloves, with wet hands, or immediately after applying hand lotion.
Multiple Kindle Fire apps running	If you have multiple apps running on your Fire tablet, quit unused apps.
Restart needed	Restarting your device involves turning it off completely and then turning it back on again. Restart your device from the **Power** dialog or **Settings** menu: <ul><li>**Fire tablets**: Press and hold the power button for two to three seconds until you see the message "Do you want to shut down your Kindle?" appear, and then tap **Shut Down**. After the device has completely turned off, press the power button to restart your Fire.</li><li>**eReaders**: From **Home**, select the **Menu** icon, and then select **Settings**. From **Settings**, select the **Menu** icon again, and then select **Restart device**.</li></ul>
Reset needed	If you continue to experience slowness after restarting your device, try resetting your device by selecting **Reset Device** from the **Settings** menu. Important: Resetting your device will remove your personal information (including your settings for Parental Controls), Amazon account information, and

any downloaded content. Any content you purchased from Amazon is automatically saved to the Cloud and can be downloaded again when you register your Fire or Kindle to your account again.

FIRE TABLET APPS

Change the Date and Time

After you connect to a wireless network and register your Fire Tablet, your Fire Tablet automatically chooses the time zone, which sets the date and time on your device. The current time is shown in the Status Bar at the top of the screen.

Note: Selecting the time zone is how you set the date and time on your Fire Tablet device. There is no option to set the date and time manually.

To change the time zone:

1. Swipe down from the top of the screen and then tap Settings.

2. Tap Device Options, and then tap Date & Time.

3. If Automatic Time Zone is turned On, your device will use a Wi-Fi or Mobile network (if available for the device) to determine the time zone. If you want to select your time zone manually, tap Off next to Automatic Time Zone, and then tap Select Time Zone. Select your time zone from the list that appears.

The clock will update to the date and time for that zone.

Use the Clock app

With the Clock app, you can set an alarm, view the time across multiple time zones, and access additional clock features like the stopwatch or timer.

To do this...	Do this...
Open the Clock app	From **Home**, tap **Apps**, and then tap **Clock**.
Add or remove a clock	Swipe from the ledge edge of the screen and tap **All Cities**. Tap ✚, and then select a city from the list, or type the name of the city you want to add. To remove a clock, press and hold the city, and then tap **Remove**.
Set an alarm	Swipe from the left edge of the screen, and then tap **Alarms**. Tap ✚ to add a new alarm. Select the time, schedule, and alarm sound, and then tap **Set Alarm**.
Set a timer	Swipe from the left edge of the screen, and then tap **Timer**. Set the timer, and then tap **Start**. When the timer is finished, it will beep until you double-tap the screen. While the timer is going, you can add additional time by tapping **Add 1 Minute**, pause the timer, or cancel the current timer.
Use a stopwatch	Swipe from the left edge of the screen, tap **Stopwatch**, and then tap **Start**. To start a new lap, tap **Lap**. To reset the stopwatch, tap **Stop**, and then tap **Reset**.
Use Nightstand	Nightstand mode will display the current time against a black background, and is ideal to use when you're sleeping. To use nightstand mode, swipe from the left edge of the screen, and then tap **Nightstand**. Tap the screen to exit Nightstand mode.

Weather

Use the Weather app on your Fire Tablet to get the current temperature, hourly forecast for the next 12 hours, and 10-day forecast for your

current location and other cities around the world.

Note: The Weather app requires a network connection.

To do this...	Do this...
Add a location	1. Tap the + icon in the upper right corner. 2. Enter the name of a city or a zip code, and then select the desired location from the search results.
View the hourly forecast for the next 12 hours	In portrait mode, the forecast for the next 9 hours is displayed at the bottom of the screen. Turn your device to landscape mode, or tap to expand the section and view the next 12 hours.
View the 10-day forecast	At the bottom of the screen tap **Daily**, and then tap to expand the section and view the forecast for the next 10 days.
View your saved locations	Swipe left or right, or swipe from the left edge of the screen and select a city from the list.
Remove a location	Swipe from the left edge of the screen, press and hold a city, and then tap **Remove**.
Manage settings, such as displaying temperature in Fahrenheit or Celsius	1. Swipe from the left edge of the screen and then tap **Settings**. 2. Modify your desired settings, and then tap the arrow to go back to the Weather app.

Browser Basics

To open the Silk browser on your Fire tablet, tap Web from the navigation bar on the Home screen.

Note: An Internet connection is required to browse the web.

The Home page appears when you open a new browser tab. From here, you can tap a website that you visit the most, or tap the address bar to search for a website. If you close the Silk browser, the last website you were viewing will automatically appear the next time you open the browser.

To do this...	Do this...
Search the web	

To do this...	Do this...
	1. Enter a URL or search term in the search field at the top of the page. Silk will suggest sites based on the default search engine you've selected. 2. Tap one of the suggested websites to go it, or tap Go on the keyboard when you're finished typing.
Zoom in and out of a web page	• To zoom in, pinch outward with two fingers. You can also double-tap with one finger to center and zoom in. • To zoom out, pinch inward with two fingers. **Note:** Some web pages do not support this functionality.
Scroll up and down on a web page	Swipe your finger up and down the screen to scroll.
Add or close a tab	• To add a new tab, tap the **+** icon. • To close a tab, tap the **x** on a tab.
• Enter private browsing • Bookmark a page • Share a page • Print a page • Change view	While viewing a web page, tap the **Menu** ⋮ icon, and then tap: • **Enter / Exit Private Browsing** - Pages you view when using Private Browsing will be removed from your browser's history after you exit Private Browsing. • **Add / Remove Bookmark** - Add a bookmark, or remove an existing bookmark, for the web page. • **Share** - Share the page via email or a social network. • **Print** - Connect to a wireless printer to print the web page from your device. • **Request Desktop Site / Mobile Site** - Select to view the Desktop or Mobile version of a web page. **Tip:** Select **Request Mobile Site** for a mobile-optimized experience. Websites that are optimized for mobile devices provide a better browsing experience by removing incompatible plug-ins and decreasing web page load times.
View bookmarks, downloads, and history	Swipe from the left edge of the screen, and then tap **Bookmarks**, **Downloads**, or **History**. **Tip:** To read a webpage offline later, long press on the link of the webpage you want to save and select **Download Link**. You can access saved webpages from **Downloads** by swiping from the left edge of the screen.

To do this...	Do this...
View a web page in Reading View	Reading View removes most graphics, advertisements, or links from a web article so you can enjoy your web articles without distractions.

- To switch to Reading View, tap the **Reading View** 📖 icon.
- To change the font size, background color, and font, tap the **Menu** ⋮ icon and select **Reading View Settings**.
- To exit Reading View, tap the **Close Reading View** 📖 icon.

Browser Settings

You can change Silk Browser settings, such as privacy controls or the default search engine, to customize your browsing experience on your Fire tablet.

To access settings for the Silk Browser, swipe from the left edge of the screen, and then tap Settings.

Setting	Description
Search Engine	Select Bing, Google, or Yahoo! as your default search engine.
Autofill Forms	Fill out your contact information on web forms with a single touch by saving form data for later use.
Save Passwords	Select this option to save your user names and passwords for websites that you visit often.

Setting	Description
Accessibility	Adjust text scaling and zoom options.
Privacy	<ul><li>**Do Not Track** - Enable this setting to request that websites not display ads based on your browsing and search history. Websites may choose to ignore these requests.</li><li>**Clear Browser Data** - Control your privacy by deleting your browser history, including websites you've visited, saved passwords, and personal information added to forms.</li></ul>
Cloud Features	Allow Silk to use the Amazon Cloud for Backup & Restore of your Silk bookmarks and preferences.
Site Settings	<ul><li>**Cookies** - Cookies are enabled by default, but you can turn them off and on. **What is a cookie?:** Cookies are small packets of data sent from a website and stored in the browser when you visit the website. Cookies retain user information (such as your preferences or settings), so that the next time you visit a website, you can pick up from where you left off (for example, proceeding to checkout on Amazon with items left in your cart from a previous browsing session).</li><li>**Location** - Allow sites to request access to your location. When a website wants to use your location data, Silk will prompt you at the bottom of the page. Tap Allow to send your location data to the website, or tap Decline to ignore the request.</li><li>**Camera** - Allow sites to request access to your camera. When a website wants to use your camera, Silk will prompt you at the bottom of the page. Tap Allow, or tap Decline to ignore the request.</li><li>**Microphone** - Allow sites to request access to your microphone. When a website wants to use your microphone, Silk will prompt you at the bottom of the page. Tap Allow, or tap Decline to ignore the request.</li><li>**Notifications** - Allow sites to display notifications.</li><li>**Images** - Allow sites to display images.</li><li>**Javascript** - Javascript allows interactive elements to appear on a website. When you disable this option, some websites may not work properly.</li><li>**Pop-ups** - Allow or block pop-up windows.</li><li>**Fullscreen** - Allow or require a prompt for sites to switch to fullscreen view.</li><li>**Protected Content** - Some websites will ask you to identify your device before you can access certain content. You can block this if you do not want your device identified but you will not be able to access this content.</li></ul>

Setting	Description

- **Storage** - View the amount of storage space that various websites are using on your device with cookies and local data, and clear and reset.

About Flash Videos on Fire Tablet

Adobe Flash isn't supported in the Silk browser, but you may be able to view Adobe Flash videos using these tips.

Adobe is no longer developing Flash for mobile devices. Due to this, the Silk Browser on Fire Tablet does not have Adobe Flash support. If you see an error message, a Flash plugin icon, or an option to redirect to a non-Flash or mobile version of the page you're viewing, this may mean that the website uses Adobe Flash.

If you're unable to view a website with Flash content, you can switch to mobile view to see if that solves your problem:

1.From the Silk web browser, tap the Menu ⋮ icon.

2.Tap Request Mobile View.
Some popular websites may also have an app available. Check the Amazon Appstore, accessible through the Apps or Games library on your device, for availability.

Media

Buy Digital Music on Fire Tablet

You can explore and purchase new music from the Digital Music Store on your Fire tablet.

Note: Digital Music Store purchases are stored in Your Music Library for free, don't count against any storage limits, and are available for playback or download on any Fire tablet, Fire phone, PC, Mac or compatible mobile device. If you want to add music from your computer to the Cloud on your Fire Tablet, you can import up to 250 songs to Your Music Library for free. You can also upgrade your Amazon Music account to import up to 250,000 songs From Home, tap Music, swipe from the left edge of the screen, and then tap Store.

1. From Home, tap Music, swipe from the left edge of the screen, and then tap Store.
2. Use the Search ⌕ tool to find a specific song, artist, album, or genre, or choose a category to browse for music.
3. To place your order, tap the button displaying the price. Tap Buy (for songs) or Buy Now (for albums) to confirm your purchase.

Tip:
- To listen to a sample, tap the song title while viewing the album details or tap the Sample this Album button on the product detail page. Song samples are limited to 30 seconds.

○ To purchase Prime Music songs, tap the More Options ⁞ icon, and then tap Buy song. In the Purchase notification, tap the Buy button to complete your purchase.

4. After purchasing your music, tap See Song in Library or See Album in Library to listen to your music, or tap Continue shopping to find more music to purchase.

Add Prime Music on Fire Tablet

If you have an Amazon Prime membership, you can stream songs, albums, and playlists from the Prime Music catalog and add them to Your Music Library on your Fire tablet for free.

Prime Music can be streamed, downloaded to your Fire tablet for offline playback, and added to your personal playlists as long as your Amazon Prime membership is active. If your Amazon Prime subscription is canceled, Prime Music songs and features on your Fire tablet and any other eligible Prime Music devices will become inaccessible to you.

Tip: You can now access Prime Stations to stream music from your Fire tablet. Prime Stations are genre-based streaming music stations you can use to discover songs from the Prime Music catalog. From your music library, swipe from the left edge of the screen and tap Prime Music, and then select Stations to get started. To add Prime Music to Your Music Library:

Manage Your Music

Music purchased from the Digital Music Store, added from the Prime Music catalog, imported to your Amazon Music Library from your computer, or transferred to your Fire tablet with a USB cable can be found in Your Music Library.

- To find music, swipe from the left edge of the screen, and then tap **Library**. Select **Playlists**, **Artists**, **Albums**, **Songs**, or **Genres**.
- To download a song, album, or playlist, tap the **More Options** icon next to the item, and then select **Download**. To cancel the download, swipe down from the top of the screen and then tap the **X**.
  Note: Prime Music can be downloaded to your device and played offline as long as your Amazon Prime membership is active.

- To delete music from your device, tap the **More Options** icon next to the item, and then tap **Remove from Device**.
- To remove music from the Cloud, tap the **More Options** icon next to the item, and then tap **Delete from Cloud** (for purchased music) or **Remove from Library** (for Prime Music). Paid music removed from your library will need to be purchased again from the Digital Music Store.
- To create a playlist, tap the **More Options** icon next to a song or an album in Your Music Library, and then select **Add to Playlist**. You can choose an existing playlist in your library or create a new playlist.

Note:

○ You can also create a playlist from the Playlists screen. Tap **+ Create a New Playlist**, enter the name of your playlist, and then tap **Save**.
○ You can't edit a Prime Playlist added to Your Music Library, but you can add Prime Music to your personal playlists.

Swipe from the left edge of the screen, and then tap Prime Music.

1.Select Stations, Playlists, Songs, or Albums.

2.Browse and select the Prime Music you want to add to Your Music Library. Eligible Prime Music titles and playlists display the Prime badge:

3.   Tap Add (for Prime songs), Add Album to Library (for Prime albums), or Add Playlist to Library (for Prime playlists).

Note:

- Adding a Prime Playlist to your library does not add the individual songs within the playlist to your library. To add individual songs from a Prime Playlist in your library, tap the Add ⊞ icon on each song row or tap the More Options ⁞ icon and select Add All Songs to Library.
- To find Prime Music you've added to your library, swipe from the left edge of the screen, and then tap Library.

Listen to Your Music

Music in your library can be played offline or streamed from the Cloud on your Fire Tablet.

Note: You may be required to authorize your device when you use Your Music Library on Fire Tablet. Authorization is required based on our license agreements with the content providers.

You can browse by playlists, artists, albums, songs, or genres, or find recently played or added music, in Your Music Library. To listen to music, tap the cover art for the music you want to play, and then tap a song name or choose another playback option in menu. When you listen to music, playback controls will appear on the screen so you can customize your listening experience.

Tip:

- If you're streaming music from the Cloud, make sure you have a strong wireless connection. Buffering, or a pause while loading or playing your music, is generally caused by a slow Internet connection.

Songs in Your Music Library will also show [+Lyrics] if they support X-Ray for Music. With X-Ray for Music, lyrics are added to your song so you can follow along line-by-line. To stop the music player running in the background, please follow the steps below:

1. Open the Music player

2. Tap and hold the Album cover next to the Play/Pause button

3. From the drop-down menu, tap "Clear Player", this will the Music player from running in background

Icon	Description
⏮	Go to the previous track.
⏭	Go to the next track.
▶	Resume playback of the song.
⏸	Pause the song.
🔁	Tap **once** to repeat all songs in the album or playlist. Tap **twice** to repeat the current song over and over.
🔀	Shuffle all songs in an album or playlist.
🔊	Adjust the volume. Alternatively, use the hardware volume controls on your device to raise or lower the volume.

SETTINGS & SECURITY

Set Up Parental Controls

Turn on Parental Controls to restrict access to certain features on your Fire Tablet, such as web browsing or purchasing from the Amazon Appstore.

From the Parental Controls screen, you can choose to create a profile in Amazon Free Time, or create a parental controls password. With Amazon Free Time, you can create a personalized profile for your child, set daily time limits, and subscribe to Amazon Free Time Unlimited to gain access to exclusive kid-friendly content for a monthly fee.

1. Swipe down from the top of the screen and then tap Settings.

2. Tap Parental Controls.

3. Tap On next to Parental Controls.

4. With Parental Controls turned on, enter a password, confirm your password, and then tap Submit. Once you've set a password, you can restrict one or more of the following:
   - Web browsing
   - The Email, Contacts, and Calendar apps
   - Social network sharing
   - The camera, if applicable

- The ability to purchase from the content stores on your device (for example, the Amazon Appstore)
- The ability to play movies and TV shows from Amazon Video
- Specific content types (for example, Books or Apps)
- Wireless connectivity
- Location-Based Services

After you turn on Parental Controls, a lock 🔒 icon appears at the top of the screen.

Turn On or Off Your Lock Screen Password or PIN

To prevent unauthorized access to your Fire Tablet, create a lock screen password or PIN.

When you wake your Fire Tablet from sleep mode or turn it on, the lock screen appears. Your lock screen displays the current time, date, and any active incoming notifications. If you have multiple household profiles on your device, you can tap your profile icon to switch profiles.

Important: If you have Amazon Free Time profiles enabled on your device, a lock screen password or PIN cannot be turned off because it is required to prevent children from accessing the adult profile.

On the lock screen, swipe down from the top of the screen to view recent notifications. You can configure your Fire Tablet so that you will be prompted to enter your lock screen password or PIN when you select a notification or slide to unlock the screen.

1. **Swipe down from the top of the screen and then tap Settings.**

2. **Tap Security & Privacy.**

3. **Next to Lock Screen Password, tap On. You can create a Simple Numeric PIN, or create a more secure password with a combination**

of letters, numbers, and special characters. Complex passwords with a combination of letters, numbers, and special characters provide more security and make it more difficult for unauthorized users to gain access to your Fire Tablet.

Factory Reset Your Fire Tablet

Reset your Fire Tablet only if you want to remove all content downloaded to it and register it again.

Before you begin, be sure to back up your device.

Important: Resetting your device will remove all content downloaded to it. Any content that is already saved to the Cloud will remain in the Cloud. You can download that content again if you register your device to your Amazon account again.

To reset you're Fire Tablet:

Swipe down from the top of the screen and tap Settings.

1. **Tap Device Options, and then tap Reset to Factory Defaults.**

2. **Tap Reset to confirm.**

Notes

Notes